U.S. Regions

The Natural Environment of the Southwest

Blaine Wiseman

MEDIA ENHANCED BOOKS
AV2 BY WEIGL
ADDED VALUE • AUDIO VISUAL

www.av2books.com

AV² provides enriched content that supplements and complements this book. Weigl's AV² books strive to create inspired learning and engage young minds in a total learning experience.

Your AV² Media Enhanced books come alive with...

Audio
Listen to sections of the book read aloud.

Key Words
Study vocabulary, and complete a matching word activity.

Video
Watch informative video clips.

Quizzes
Test your knowledge.

Go to **www.av2books.com**, and enter this book's unique code.

BOOK CODE

N339679

Embedded Weblinks
Gain additional information for research.

Slide Show
View images and captions, and prepare a presentation.

AV² **by Weigl** brings you media enhanced books that support active learning.

Try This!
Complete activities and hands-on experiments.

... and much, much more!

Published by AV² by Weigl
350 5th Avenue, 59th Floor
New York, NY 10118

Websites: www.av2books.com   www.weigl.com

Library of Congress Control Number: 2014942129

ISBN 978-1-4896-1238-0 (hardcover)
ISBN 978-1-4896-1239-7 (softcover)
ISBN 978-1-4896-1240-3 (single-user eBook)
ISBN 978-1-4896-1241-0 (multi-user eBook)

Printed in the United States of America in North Mankato, Minnesota
1 2 3 4 5 6 7 8 9 18 17 16 15 14

062014
WEP090514

Project Coordinator: Aaron Carr
Design: Mandy Christiansen

Every reasonable effort has been made to trace ownership and to obtain permission to reprint copyright material. The publishers would be pleased to have any errors or omissions brought to their attention so that they may be corrected in subsequent printings.

Weigl acknowledges Getty Images as its primary image supplier for this title.

Contents

U.S. Regions

The United States is made up of five major regions. These areas are made of natural landforms. Each region also offers its own mix of land, **climates**, animals, and plants. Many different environments exist within each region.

Legend

- West (11 states)
- Southwest (5 states)
- Northeast (11 states)
- Southeast (11 states)
- Midwest (12 states)

Washington

Oregon

Montana

Idaho

Nevada

Wyoming

Utah

California

Colorado

Arizona

New Mexico

Pacific Ocean

MEXICO

The Southwest borders the West, the Midwest, the Southeast, Mexico, and the Gulf of Mexico.

The Southwest covers 617,341 square miles (1,598,905 square kilometers).

Alaska

0   500 Miles
0   500 Kilometers

Hawai'i

0   100 Miles
0   100 Kilometers

CANADA

North
Dakota

Minnesota

Lake
Superior

New
Hampshire

Maine

Vermont

South
Dakota

Wisconsin

Lake
Huron

Massachusetts

Lake Ontario

New York

Lake
Michigan

Michigan

Lake Erie

Rhode
Island

Nebraska

Iowa

Illinois

Indiana

Ohio

Pennsylvania

New
Jersey

Connecticut

UNITED STATES

West
Virginia

Virginia

Delaware

Maryland

Kansas

Missouri

Kentucky

North Carolina

Oklahoma

Arkansas

Tennessee

South
Carolina

Texas

Mississippi

Alabama

Georgia

Atlantic
Ocean

Louisiana

N

Florida

Gulf of Mexico

0   250 Miles

0   250 Kilometers

What Makes the Southwest?

The Southwest is known for its varied, rugged landscapes. In Colorado, the Rocky Mountains tower above the Great Plains. This mountain range, North America's largest, extends through the western United States and Canada. New Mexico is mostly dry land. It includes vast deserts, deep canyons, high **mesas**, and dusty **arroyos**. Oklahoma stretches across the Great Plains. It is home to prairies, swamps, forests, **plateaus**, and mountain areas. The Ozark Mountains cross from Oklahoma into Arkansas before the land flattens out into the Arkansas River Valley. Large rivers flow south to the **Gulf** of Mexico.

After Alaska, Texas is the largest state in the country. Texas covers almost half of the Southwest region. Its largest distance measures 801 miles (1,289 kilometers) from east to west and 773 miles (1,244 km) from north to south. Texas includes a long gulf coastline and islands, plains, and mountains. The Rio Grande divides Texas from the country of Mexico to the southwest. *Rio Grande* is Spanish for "Great River."

🍃 Cougars are also called mountain lions, pumas, and panthers. Growing cougar populations are found in Colorado, New Mexico, and Texas.

Major Landmarks of the Southwest

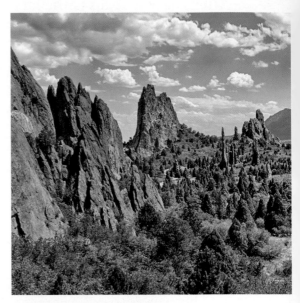

The land in the Southwest has been formed over a very long time by weather, volcanoes, and flowing water. These changes continue to occur, slowly building more landforms. Oklahoma was at the bottom of the ocean millions of years ago. When the land rose higher, that ocean left behind the salt that now makes up the Great Salt Plains. The area is protected for animals such as the **endangered** whooping crane. Plants do not grow in the salty ground.

Colorado, Garden of the Gods
Garden of the Gods is a public park owned by the city of Colorado Springs. It offers towering sandstone rock formations. Many hiking trails wind through the park.

Digging for crystals at the Great Salt Plains requires a permit.

New Mexico, Ship Rock

Ship Rock stands 1,400 feet (430 meters) above the plains on the Navajo Nation. It is the interior rock of a volcano that erupted about 30 million years ago.

Texas, Palo Duro Canyon

The second-largest canyon in the United States is Palo Duro Canyon. It has been carved over 90 million years by weather and the rushing waters of the Red River. *Palo duro* means "hard wood" in Spanish.

Arkansas, Mammoth Spring

Mammoth Spring starts more than 80 feet (24 m) below the ground and flows to the surface. About 9 million gallons (34 million liters) of water flow from the spring every hour. The water forms a lake and a river.

Oklahoma,
Great Salt Plains

The Great Salt Plains Wildlife Refuge protects more than 300 species, or types, of birds.

People have collected salt from the Great Salt Plains for thousands of years.

The Great Salt Plains is the only place in the world where there are hourglass-shaped crystals of salt.

Major Biomes of the Southwest

The largest communities of plants and animals are called biomes. Each species in a biome, including humans, plays a role. Protecting the world's biomes is an important part of **conserving** its environment. The Southwest is made up of four major biomes.

Mapping the Biomes of the Southwest

Use the map below and the information on the next page to answer the following questions.

1. How many states have a **deciduous** forest biome?
2. Which states have a coniferous forest biome?
3. How many states have a desert biome?

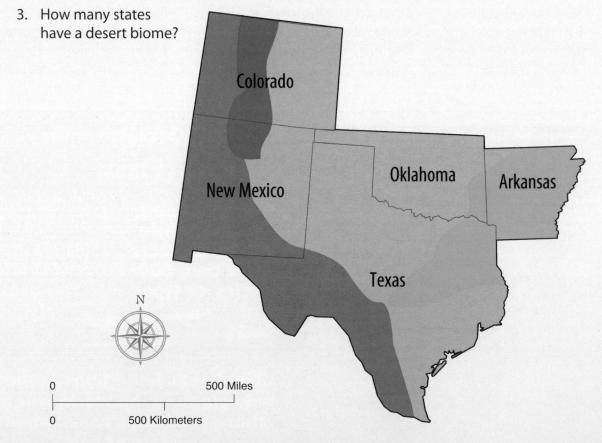

Deciduous Forest

Climate: Seasonal
Vegetation: Dense leafy trees, flowers
Temperature: -22° to 86° Fahrenheit
(-30° to 30° Celsius)

Coniferous Forest

Climate: Seasonal
Vegetation: Evergreen trees
Temperature: -4° to 104° F
(-20° to 40° C)

Grasslands

Climate: Dry, seasonal
Vegetation: Grasses
Temperature: -4° to 86° F
(-20° to 30° C)

Desert

Climate: Hot, dry
Vegetation: Water-retaining plants, cactus plants
Temperature: 0° to 120° F (-18° to 49° C)

The mountain goat climbs the Rocky Mountains of Colorado to find grasses, herbs, shrubs, ferns, and mosses to eat.

Ecosystems of the Southwest

A biome contains smaller communities called ecosystems. Plants, animals, and nonliving things, such as air, soil, and water, create an ecosystem. Ecosystems can be large or small. In the Southwest, within the large desert biome are many smaller ecosystems. Cactus plants, birds, snakes, and other plants and animals rely on one another and the weather to survive. One ecosystem within the desert is called an **oasis**. Trees and fish that could not survive in the dry desert can survive in an oasis.

Food for Thought

The plants and animals in an ecosystem are part of a food cycle. Through the food cycle, the **organisms** in an ecosystem pass **nutrients** to each other. Plants get their nutrients from the Sun and the soil. Then, **herbivores** eat those plants full of nutrients. The same nutrients now pass to the **carnivores** feeding on those animals. When an animal dies, its body decays, or breaks down, adding chemicals to the soil. Those chemicals help the plant make nutrients. In this way, the food cycle starts again.

Food Cycle

A prickly pear cactus begins the food cycle by making nutrients from the Sun and soil.

Insects eat the seeds and fruit of the cactus.

Roadrunners eat the insects for the nutrients. They pass the nutrients on to a **predator** or back to the soil when they die.

Major Rivers of the Southwest

Rivers have had a major part in shaping the Southwest. Many of the region's longest rivers start in Colorado or New Mexico. From the eastern side of the Rocky Mountains, these powerful rivers create canyons, gorges, valleys, and borders along the way. Most of the rivers flowing through the Southwest end at the Gulf of Mexico.

Colorado, Rio Grande
The Rio Grande is 1,900 miles (3,058 km) long. It begins as a stream created by melting snow along the Continental Divide. The series of mountain ridges that stretch from Alaska to Mexico and separate two different river systems is called the Continental Divide. The Rio Grande flows across New Mexico to Texas.

Arkansas, Arkansas River
This body of water flows 1,460 miles (2,350 km) from Colorado to Arkansas. In Oklahoma, it joins with the 906-mile (1,458-km) Canadian River before flowing into the Mississippi River.

Oklahoma, Red River

The Red River runs 1,290 miles (2,080 km). Half of the river acts as the border between Oklahoma and Texas. The waterway gets its name from the large amounts of red soil that it carries from the surrounding plains.

Texas, Brazos River

Two separate streams flow more than 150 miles (240 km) before joining to form the Brazos River. The 1,280-mile (2,060-km) river used to be called the *Brazos de Dios*, which means "arms of god" in Spanish.

New Mexico, Pecos River

From the mountains of New Mexico, the Pecos flows 926 miles (1,490 km). It is a **tributary** of the Rio Grande. For much of the year, the river runs dry in the heat of the New Mexico desert.

River Facts

The Rio Grande **DROPS 12,000 feet** (3,658 m) from the Rocky Mountains to the Gulf of Mexico.

In the Southwest, rivers on the east side of the Continental Divide
- - - - - - - - - - - - - -
flow to the Gulf of Mexico. Rivers on the west side flow to the Pacific Ocean.

In Mexico, the Rio Grande is known as Rio Bravo del Norte. That is Spanish for *"wild river of the North."*

N

The Red River was a tributary of the Mississippi River until a dam was built in 1963.

Mammals of the Southwest

The Southwest region is home to a variety of **mammals**. The wide-open spaces and unique ecosystems of the region help these mammals survive, but many are still in trouble. Humans have changed the region's natural areas. There are endangered land and sea mammals in the Southwest, such as jaguars, manatees, and humpback whales.

Texas and Oklahoma, Mexican Free-tailed Bat
Mexican free-tailed bats live in the largest mammal group in the world. A single group, or colony, in Texas has about 20 million bats.

Arkansas, White-tailed Deer
The white-tailed deer can run 40 miles (60 km) per hour. They use their white tails like a flag to warn other deer of danger.

Texas, Texas Longhorn
The Texas Longhorn is the official large mammal of Texas. Its horns can grow to more than 6 feet (1.8 m) long. In the past, this type of cattle roamed free. Today, longhorns live on farms and ranches.

Colorado, Rocky Mountain Bighorn Sheep
The horns of Rocky Mountain bighorn sheep are made of bone. These curly horns can grow up to 50 inches (130 centimeters) in length, and weigh up to 30 pounds (14 kilograms).

Texas, Nine-banded Armadillo

The nine-banded armadillo is the official small mammal of Texas. Related to the sloth and the anteater, it is North America's only armadillo species. If attacked, armadillos roll into a ball, using their hard shells for protection.

New Mexico, Black Bear

Black bears are not always black. They can be the color of cinnamon, beige, grey, or even white. Their diet includes animals and plants, such as fruits, roots, and pinecones. Black bears can weigh as much as 600 pounds (270 kg).

Oklahoma, American Bison

The American bison, sometimes called buffaloes, measure 6 feet (1.8 m) tall and weigh up to 1,800 pounds (800 kg). Millions of bison roamed the plains in large herds before settlers hunted them. Today, they live in protected areas in the United States and Canada.

Reptiles and Amphibians of the Southwest

Reptiles and amphibians are cold-blooded animals. That means they have a body temperature that changes with the environment's temperature. Large numbers of reptiles and amphibians live in wet and dry areas of the Southwest. In the dry areas, reptiles feed on plants, insects, birds, small mammals, and small reptiles. Other reptiles, larger mammals, and birds, in turn, eat them. Snakes, lizards, and turtles are reptiles. Amphibians live around the many rivers, lakes, swamps, and coastal areas of the region. They lay their eggs in or near these waters. Salamanders, frogs, and toads are amphibians.

American alligators *have existed for more than* **150 million years**.

Pit vipers *have pits in their heads that sense heat, helping them hunt.*

Unofficial State Reptiles

Arkansas, Western Cottonmouth		The Western cottonmouth is a pit viper. It uses powerful venom, or poison, to kill its prey. This reptile usually lives and hunts near the water.
Texas, American Alligator		American alligators are found in or near water, usually by the Gulf Coast. They can weigh up to 1,000 pounds (450 kg). American alligators feed on fish, turtles, various mammals, birds, and other reptiles.
Texas, Texas Tortoise		In the past, Texas tortoises were popular as pets, causing the population in nature to decline. Today, this tortoise is a threatened species in Texas.

Official State Reptiles

Colorado, Western Painted Turtle

The western painted turtle is an omnivore, which means it feeds on both plants and animals. During the winter months, it **hibernates**.

New Mexico, New Mexico Whiptail Lizard

All New Mexico whiptail lizards are females. With no males to mate with, they must produce **offspring** by themselves.

Oklahoma, Collared Lizard

Collared lizards have black bands that look like a collar. They are also sometimes called mountain boomers.

Texas, Texas Horned Lizard

The horned lizard was a symbol of health and happiness to ancient American Indians in the Southwest. Today, this reptile is a **threatened** species in Texas.

Official State Amphibians

New Mexico, New Mexico Spadefoot Toad

The New Mexico spadefoot toad is named for its sharp back feet. It gets moisture from the soil by digging with these feet.

Oklahoma, Bullfrog

The bullfrog is the largest frog in North America. It makes loud noises that scare off predators.

Birds of the Southwest

Many types of birds live throughout the Southwest. Some species stop to rest and feed here on their long **migrations**. Others stay in this region all year long. Grasslands and forests are perfect territories for birds, with a variety of plants and animals to eat. Some birds in the Southwest are at home in the desert. The Eskimo curlew is an endangered bird species from the Southwest. In fact, experts believe it may have died out.

New Mexico, Greater Roadrunner
The greater roadrunner is also known as the chaparral bird. Roadrunners are a type of cuckoo bird. They can fly but spend most of their time on the ground.

Greater roadrunners use their speed and power to hunt prey such as lizards, other birds, and even rattlesnakes.

A mockingbird can learn up to 200 different songs during its life.

Scientists have not seen an Eskimo curlew in nature since 1963.

Arkansas and Texas, Northern Mockingbird
The mockingbird gets its name because it can mock, or mimic, sounds. Mockingbirds are known to copy the sounds of other birds, insects, animals, and even machines.

Colorado, Lark Bunting
The lark bunting is a type of sparrow. When it is time to mate, the male sings and dances in the sky to attract a female. The **breeding** male is all black with white wings. Otherwise, they are grayish brown.

Texas, Barn Owl

Barn owls live in almost every region of the United States. These owls sleep all day in dark, quiet places, such as old barns. Owls do not chew their food but swallow it whole.

Oklahoma,
Scissor-tailed Flycatcher

The scissor-tailed flycatcher eats insects that can destroy farm crops. Its tail, which looks like a pair of scissors, can be twice as long as its body.

Scissor-tailed flycatchers sometimes build their nests using string, paper, and bits of carpet.

In the 1930s, wild turkeys nearly died out. Today, there are more than 6 million across the United States.

During mating season, a male Colorado bluebird can sing up to 1,000 songs per hour.

Oklahoma, Wild Turkey

The wild turkey is Oklahoma's official **game bird**. It can grow up to 4 feet (1.2 m) tall and weigh more than 20 pounds (9 kg).

Plants of the Southwest

The Southwest is home to thousands of plant species. High in the Rocky Mountains, huge pine trees grow beside tiny mosses covering rocks and logs. In the desert, some of the few plants that can grow without much water are cactus plants and small shrubs. The plains are covered in fields of grass that stretch for thousands of miles (km). Rivers, lakes, swamps, and the Gulf of Mexico support many types of plant life, such as **algae** and vines.

Colorado
White and lavender rocky mountain columbine grows near the bottom of mountains. It is protected by the state of Colorado.

The word for more than one cactus is *cacti*.

Early settlers in New Mexico used yucca as food, firewood, and even soap.

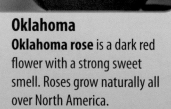

Oklahoma
Oklahoma rose is a dark red flower with a strong sweet smell. Roses grow naturally all over North America.

Colorado and New Mexico
Blue grama grass can take as long as 50 years to grow back if it has been plowed up in an area.

New Mexico
Yucca has more than 40 different species. Most yucca species have white flowers.

Oklahoma
Redbud is a small tree with bright pink blossoms. It grows to a height of 30 feet (9 m).

Arkansas
Apple blossoms are the pink and white flowers of apple trees. When a bee, wasp, or other insect transfers **pollen** from one apple blossom to another, an apple can grow.

Arkansas
Loblolly pine trees are sometimes called Arkansas pine. These trees can reach a height of more than 100 feet (30 m). They are often used to make telephone poles.

A pecan tree can produce nuts for more than 300 years.

The cochineal, a type of insect that feeds on the prickly pear cactus, is used to make red food coloring.

Texas
Prickly pear cactus can grow as tall as 7 feet (2 m). The people of the Southwest have eaten the pear, the flower petals, and the pads of the cactus for thousands of years.

Colorado
Colorado blue spruce is also sometimes called the silver spruce. The color of this tree's branches can be blue, green, or silver.

Texas
Pecan trees can survive for more than 1,000 years. Some of them grow taller than 100 feet (30 m) high.

Challenges Facing the Southwest

The Southwest's natural areas are affected by many things. When the region's natural climate is paired with a weather event, it has a major impact on the plants, animals, and people. For example, in the early 1930s, hot weather with little rain over time caused the grassland areas in the Southwest to dry out. The grasses and crops that had covered the region died. They were replaced with dry, dusty soil. The weather continued, and winds carried the dust across the country. Today, **drought**, wildfires, flooding, and various human activities continue to challenge the region.

🌿 In Texas, severe droughts have caused shortages of grass, hay, and water. Without food and water for their herds, ranchers risk losing cattle.

Human Impact

A lack of natural water is a challenge for the Southwest. People need water for drinking and use in their homes. Farmers use water to grow their crops. Other groups, such as the oil and gas industries, require water to operate in the Southwest. Plants and animals in the grasslands, deserts, and forests also need water to survive. Human activities such as housing construction, mowing fields, and building roads can damage these natural **habitats**. Some organizations and concerned people are working to protect the ecosystems of the Southwest.

In 2012, land all over the Southwest dried up, and farm crops died.

Water

Communities in the Southwest get their water from rivers, large human-made lakes called reservoirs, and underground streams. These sources are in danger of drying up. This would affect millions of people, as well as animals.

In 2012, the worst **DROUGHT** hit the United States since the 1950s.

In the Upper Rio Grande region, **75%** of the water is used by farms.

The **LARGEST** lakes in the Southwest are reservoirs.

Endangered Species Spotlight

Jaguars live in much of South America, Mexico, and parts of the United States. These large cats are most threatened in the United States. Farms, towns, and cities near the U.S.-Mexican border have destroyed large parts of the jaguar's natural habitat. This makes it difficult for the big cats to hunt and migrate. Today, fewer than 100 jaguars live in the area.

The Texas blind salamander lives in the water of underground caves in a small area of Texas. It lives in complete darkness and hunts by sensing the movement of its prey in the water. Water pollution and low water levels are the biggest threats to the Texas blind salamander.

Jaguars are the third-largest cats in the world, after tigers and lions.

The whooping crane, which stands as tall as 5 feet (1.5 m), is the tallest bird in North America. In 1941, only 16 whooping cranes existed in the world. The greatest threats to these birds have been loss of their habitats to farming, illegal hunting, and power lines. The U.S. and Canadian governments began working with scientists on a **breeding program**. Scientists even helped guide the birds on their migrations using small light aircraft. One group travels more than 2,500 miles (4,000 km) between northern Canada and the Gulf Coast in Texas. Today, about 400 whooping cranes live in their natural habitats.

The Texas blind salamander has no eyes.

Get Involved

Organizations all over the United States are working for the recovery of endangered species. These organizations support the protection of habitats, help injured animals, and teach the public about endangered species. They also work with the government to create special areas and laws that protect wildlife, such as the jaguar.

Protecting the natural habitat of the jaguar is the most important step to help the animal survive in the United States. You can volunteer to help a conservation group such as Defenders of Wildlife. Talk to your classmates, teachers, and family about donating money to help care for a jaguar, or sign up to help teach people. You can also write a letter to members of your local, state, or federal government to share your views.

For more information, visit Defenders of Wildlife at www. defenders.org/ jaguar/how-you-can-help.

Activity

Whooping cranes migrate two times a year. In the fall, they fly south to spend the winter in a warmer climate. When spring comes, the whooping cranes return north to breed. The birds can fly for more than 400 miles (600 km) without stopping. When they land, however, they need to rest and find food. Whooping cranes rely on wetland habitats, such as marshes, to survive. Wetlands provide them with fish, insects, and frogs to eat. The whooping cranes' migration would become much more difficult if wetlands along their route are destroyed.

🍃 Whooping cranes are named after the noise they make, which can be heard as far as 2 miles (3 km) away.

Map a Migration

Use this book, and research on the internet, to create a map of the whooping crane's 700 mile (1,000 km) journey through Oklahoma and Texas.

1. Draw or print an outline map of Oklahoma and Texas. Mark two dots to show Aransas National Wildlife Refuge (NWR) in Texas and Salt Plains NWR in Oklahoma.
2. Connect the two dots with a line. This is part of the whooping crane's migration route.
3. Using a black marker, place dots to show cities along the route.
4. Using a blue marker, draw lakes, rivers, and other wetland areas along the route.
5. With your new map, locate the best places for whooping cranes to stop and rest. Remember that they need areas away from humans.
6. Now, consider what would happen to the whooping cranes if the wetlands disappeared. Write down your thoughts and share them with your classmates.

Sample Migration Map

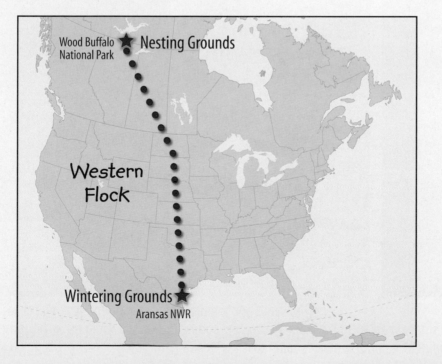

Quiz

1 What is the largest state in the United States, after Alaska?

2 What is the second-largest canyon in the United States?

3 Which large river in New Mexico flows into the Rio Grande?

4 What is the official small mammal of Texas?

5 What is North America's largest frog?

6 What coloring does a breeding male lark bunting have?

7 What bird has not been seen in nature since 1963?

8 What plant supports an insect used for food coloring?

9 What animal has no eyes and lives in underground caves in Texas?

10 How far do whooping cranes travel on their migration from Canada?

ANSWERS: 1. Texas 2. Palo Duro Canyon 3. Pecos River 4. Nine-banded armadillo 5. Bullfrog 6. All black with white wings 7. Eskimo curlew 8. Prickly pear cactus 9. Texas blind salamander 10. More than 2,500 miles (4,000 km)

Key Words

algae: organisms without roots, stems, or leaves that grow in water

arroyos: usually dry streams that fill with rainwater

breeding: creating new members of a species

breeding program: the planned breeding and raising of animal species that are at risk of dying out in their natural habitats

carnivores: animals that feed mostly on other animals

climates: the usual weather conditions in regions

conserving: protecting from harm

deciduous: losing leaves each winter

drought: a long time with little or no rain

endangered: in danger of disappearing

game bird: a bird that can be hunted

gulf: an area of an ocean or sea that is mostly surrounded by land

habitats: places where animals or plants naturally live

herbivores: animals that feeds mainly on plants

hibernates: spends the winter in an inactive state

mammals: animals that have hair or fur and drink milk from their mother

mesas: flat-topped land formations, often in the Southwest

migrations: regular movements from one region or climate to another

nutrients: substances that living things need to survive and grow

oasis: a small area in the desert with a water source

offspring: the young of a person, animal, or plant

organisms: living things

plateaus: raised areas of land with a flat top

pollen: tiny grains that help the female parts of a plant produce seeds

predator: an animal that hunts other animals for food

threatened: at risk of becoming endangered

tributary: a stream or river that flows into a larger river

Index

Log on to www.av2books.com

AV[2] by Weigl brings you media enhanced books that support active learning. Go to www.av2books.com, and enter the special code found on page 2 of this book. You will gain access to enriched and enhanced content that supplements and complements this book. Content includes video, audio, weblinks, quizzes, a slide show, and activities.

AV[2] Online Navigation

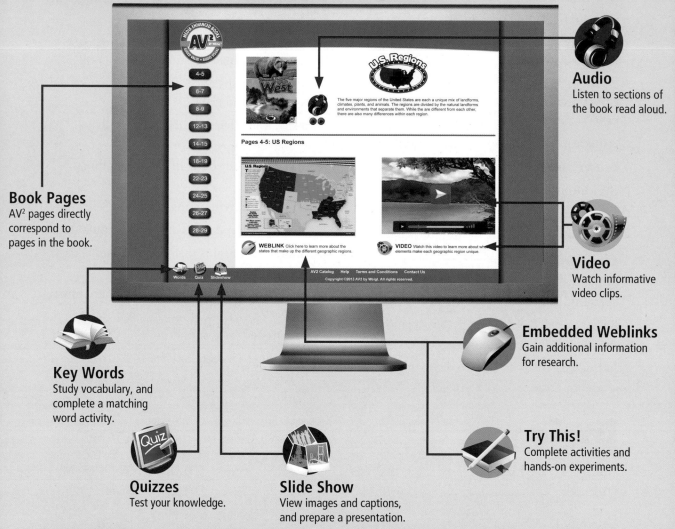

Audio
Listen to sections of the book read aloud.

Book Pages
AV[2] pages directly correspond to pages in the book.

Video
Watch informative video clips.

Embedded Weblinks
Gain additional information for research.

Key Words
Study vocabulary, and complete a matching word activity.

Try This!
Complete activities and hands-on experiments.

Quizzes
Test your knowledge.

Slide Show
View images and captions, and prepare a presentation.

AV[2] was built to bridge the gap between print and digital. We encourage you to tell us what you like and what you want to see in the future.

Sign up to be an AV[2] Ambassador at www.av2books.com/ambassador.

Due to the dynamic nature of the Internet, some of the URLs and activities provided as part of AV[2] by Weigl may have changed or ceased to exist. AV[2] by Weigl accepts no responsibility for any such changes. All media enhanced books are regularly monitored to update addresses and sites in a timely manner. Contact AV[2] by Weigl at 1-866-649-3445 or av2books@weigl.com with any questions, comments, or feedback.